Contents

EUTHANASIA – A Christian Perspective

Credits

General Editors: Hugh Brown
and Kristine Gibbs.
Design concept: Mark Blackadder.
Photographs: Walter Bell.
Typeset in Palatino and Helvetica.

Published on behalf of:
The BOARD of SOCIAL RESPONSIBILITY
of The CHURCH of SCOTLAND
by SAINT ANDREW PRESS
121 George Street, Edinburgh EH2 4YN

Copyright ©
The BOARD of SOCIAL RESPONSIBILITY
of The CHURCH of SCOTLAND 1995

British Library in Cataloguing Data
A catalogue record for this book is
available from the British Library.
ISBN 086153204X

Printed and **bound** in Scotland by:
Fingerprint (Scotland) Ltd, Livingston.

Preface

This book is based on the report of a Church of Scotland study group which was set up in 1992 with the following remit:

> *Aware of rising concern and apprehension amongst Church members and the public about euthanasia, the Board of Social Responsibility, recognising the Christian position on the sanctity of life, appoints a study group to study euthanasia, suicide and living wills and to report.*

The study group was convened by a consultant in geriatric medicine and its members were a consultant in palliative medicine, three ministers, two lawyers (one a Queen's Counsel), three social workers, and a teacher.

They completed their work and reported to the General Assembly of 1994 in the normal format of the *Blue Book* of reports to the General Assembly, and the report was commended to the attention of the membership of the Church. It was felt however that, in order to facilitate this, and because of the wider public interest of the subject matter, it should be made more widely available in a more readily readable form.

Since the Assembly of 1994 there have been further developments. The House of Lords Select Committee has reported and its recommendations have been largely accepted by the UK Government. The law has changed further in the Netherlands and the advocacy of euthanasia by the 'Right to Die' Societies continues unabated in most Western countries. The publicity effort of the Voluntary Euthanasia Societies (VES) also continues and media attention is sought in order to promote their cause at every opportunity. The debate is by no means over; the pressure to introduce deliberate killing as a treatment option for the seriously and terminally ill is being maintained and the level of commitment of those who see this as a desirable end is by no means negligible. They remain a vigorous minority and, in the absence of an opposing voice, they might succeed in achieving their aim by default.

Dr George Chalmers
Convener, Study Group on Euthanasia

Introduction

I am delighted that this book is now available to those who desire to understand a little more about euthanasia, from a Christian perspective, to those who wish to extend their knowledge and understanding of the subject, and to those who wish to put their Church's view into a more general perspective as portrayed in the press and media. I believe that this book can fulfil all these aspirations.

It is always good to see a new title added to the list of titles now available to members of the Church, other Churches, and of no Church. The objective of all the books is to facilitate informed discussion and debate on the range of issues which fall within the remit of the Board of Social Responsibility. If you find it helpful, recommend it to a friend or to someone who is confronted with this issue; it is a live subject and unfortunately it confronts people daily, often suddenly, and always when emotions are liable to take over from reasoned thinking.

If the issue has not yet confronted you personally, I trust that this book will better prepare you to deal with it when it does arise. Remember in your prayers those who are struggling with decisions about friends or relatives and euthanasia.

Ian D Baillie
Director of Social Work

EUTHANASIA
A Christian Perspective

What has the CHURCH said previously about EUTHANASIA?

Previous statements

The Church of Scotland, while in no way deficient in compassion, has taken a firm position based on the principle of the sanctity of life.

Previous deliverances from the General Assembly in the last 15 years have read as follows:

While seeing no virtue in the prolongation of dying we [The General Assembly] *are aware of no theological difficulty in allowing a patient* _in extremis_ *to die naturally, disapprove of the deliberate termination of life, and see the alternative as 'good terminal care'.* [We] *believe that legislation on the subject of euthanasia would be difficult to frame, interpret and enforce and would be open to unfortunate projections. It would be unacceptable to many doctors and would make for unhappy relationships in homes and hospitals for the aged and the long term disabled.* [We] *call upon Christians to seek alternatives to euthanasia in adequate concern for those whose life has become burdensome by reason of age and illness.* (1977)

The General Assembly re-affirms the view consistently held, that the Christian recognises no right to dispose of his own life, even though he may regard those who commit or attempt to commit suicide with compassion and understanding rather than condemnation. On the same basis of the Christian belief in God's sovereignty over life, there can be no support for the concept of the permissibility in law to kill a fellow human being even when he requests it. (1981)

'... there can be no support for the concept of the permissibility in law to kill a fellow human being even when he requests it.'

During the last decade professional, social and legal practice has changed, particularly in the Netherlands and in the USA; Private Members' Bills relating to euthanasia have been introduced in the UK Parliament and defeated; the Medical Treatment (Advanced Directives) Bill has been debated, and in February 1993 the House of Lords established a Select Committee on Medical Ethics with the remit:

> *To consider the ethical, legal and clinical implications of a person's right to withhold consent to life prolonging treatment, and the position of persons who are no longer able to give or withhold consent: and to consider whether and in what circumstances actions that have as their intention or a likely consequence the shortening of another person's life, may be justified on the grounds that they accord with that person's wishes or with that person's best interests: and in all the foregoing considerations regard is to be paid to the likely effects of changes in law or medical practice on society as a whole.*

Their Lordships' report, published and now accepted by the Government, contains conclusions and recommendations which may be summarised as follows:

1   There should be no change in the law to permit euthanasia (House of Lords report, 1993).
2   A competent patient's right to refuse consent to any medical treatment is strongly endorsed.
3   If an individual refusal of treatment by a competent patient is over-ruled by the court, full reason should be given.
4   The development and growth of palliative care services is strongly commended.
5   'Double effect' is not a reason for withholding treatment that would give relief if the doctor is acting in accordance with responsible medical practice with the object of relieving pain or distress and without the intention to kill.

'There should be no change in the law to permit euthanasia.' (House of Lords report, 1993)

6   Treatment limiting decisions should be made jointly by all involved in the care of a patient on the basis that treatment may be judged inappropriate if it will add nothing to the patient's well-being as a person.

7   Definition of Persistent Vegetative State (PVS) and a code of practice relating to its management should be developed.

8   Development and acceptance of the idea that, in certain circumstances, some treatment may be inappropriate and need not be given, should make it unnecessary in future to consider the withdrawal of nutrition and hydration, except where its administration is in itself evidently burdensome to the patient.

9   Treatment limiting decisions should not be determined by resource considerations.

10 Rejection of euthanasia as an option for the individual entails a compelling social responsibility to care adequately for those who are elderly, dying or disabled (House of Lords report, 1993).

11 Palliative care should be made more widely available.

12 Research into pain relief and symptom control should be adequately supported.

13 Training of health-care professionals should prepare them for ethical responsibility.

14 Long term care of dependent people should have special regard to maintenance of individual dignity.

15 Support is given to proposals for a new judicial forum with power to make decisions about medical treatment for incompetent patients.

16 Creation of a new offence of mercy killing is not recommended.

17 The recommendation that the mandatory life sentence for murder should be abolished is strongly endorsed.

18 No change should be made in the law on assisted suicide.

19 The development of advanced directives is commended but legislation for advance directives generally is considered unnecessary.

20 A code of practice on advance directives should be developed.

21 There should be no more widespread development of a system of proxy decision-making.

Why should we be concerned about EUTHANASIA?

Increase in the public profile of euthanasia

The rising concern and apprehension amongst Church members and the public, which was quoted as a reason for this study, results from a significant increase in the media profile of euthanasia and in general awareness and discussion. There is a media-led demand to know of the intimate details of harrowing personal tragedies, which might be better handled by doctors, relatives and carers, out of the glare of publicity. The activities of pressure groups such as the Voluntary Euthanasia Society (VES), the 'Right to Die' Societies and other vociferous, usually Humanist, minority groups, have also contributed to this increase in awareness.

Demographic changes

The national increase in the number and proportion of elderly people in the population is well documented; this is in the context of a decrease of the younger population by a falling birth rate since the second decade of the century. The overall decrease in family size has reduced the availability of potential carers for older and disabled people, throwing an ever greater load upon voluntary and statutory health-care and supportive services. In an ageing population questions are being asked about our capacity to continue care at current or increased levels, and the option of euthanasia as an 'ultimate solution' has been raised.

Sociological changes

Sociological factors may be playing a part in causing people to look at death as an option where care is difficult. These may include a decrease in family stability related to the higher prevalence of divorce and separation; increased personal and family mobility leading to diminished family and community cohesion; and an increase in dependence on statutory care.

Medical changes

Major improvements in preventive and curative medicine have not only increased the expectation of life, but have also increased the overall expectation of cure, and this in turn has diminished the acceptance of illness and even of death as part of normal human experience. While there is undoubtedly greater potential for intervention in disease (even in life-threatening situations by the use of resuscitation techniques, life support technology and pharmacological advances), there is also a higher expectation that such intervention will be universally applicable, even in some instances where it may be entirely inappropriate. The judgement to distinguish between what can be done and what should be done has become an increasingly important issue for doctors.

Several of the well publicised cases in which the issues of euthanasia have been discussed have been instances in which such judgement has been crucial. A fairly widespread fear of meddle-some medicine has lent fuel to the demand for the availability of euthanasia.

Health-care economies

Seldom discussed, but ever present as a hidden agenda, is the awareness that caring is expensive and euthanasia would be cheaper. We are reminded constantly of the difficulty in financing health-care and some people are now prepared to make public their ideas along these lines. The Church must stand on the infinite worth of the individual in a society which may easily become influenced by the cost of care.

'The Church must stand on the infinite worth of the individual in a society which may easily become influenced by the cost of care.'

Changes in the personal view of life

Increasingly, as general awareness of God's involvement with humanity seems to be diminishing, there is a loss of the concept of human life as God's gift. In the view of many, life has become an individual's right and possession, to be disposed of as they will. This has resulted in major changes in the perception of death and life after death.[1]

Changes in the language of dying

In the context of the Euthanasia debate it is interesting, and indeed disturbing, that the pressure groups seeking the introduction of voluntary euthanasia and assisted suicide tend to use language which conceals the lethal nature of the acts proposed.

> One no longer commits suicide – one performs 'self-deliverance'. A physician under a 'right to die' law would no longer give a lethal injection he would administer an 'aid in dying measure.[2]

---

1   *Lifestyle Survey:* Church of Scotland Board of Social Responsibility (Quorum Press, Edinburgh 1987).
2   *When is it right to die?:* Joni Eareckson Tada (Marshall Pickering, 1992), p 31.

Definitions

Since the Church's last report in 1981 some of the definitions and categories in this area have changed. Recent developments in particular have given rise to alterations in emphasis, in application and in attitudes.

1 Euthanasia

The original definition of *euthanasia* derived from two Greek words: *eu thanatos* – 'dying well' or 'good death'. This concept of an easy or good death is one in which the relief of symptoms is sufficient to allow the patient to continue normal relationships and cognitive thought right to the immediate pre-terminal phase of life, without the intrusion of pain or other distress. Today, **euthanasia means deliberately terminating the life of another person by an act or omission in the context of terminal, painful or distressing illness.** 'Mercy-killing' is also used, defining motivation as much as action.

Active euthanasia: is doing something positive such as giving a drug with the intention to bring about death.

Passive euthanasia: is the deliberate shortening of life through an omission to act. The term 'passive euthanasia' is applied, quite inappropriately, to treatment withdrawal, where the treatment concerned is proving ineffective in achieving recovery and should rightly be stopped. Neither the withdrawal of inappropriate treatment, nor the decision to refrain from using it, can correctly be called euthanasia. These decisions are the expression of good clinical judgement.

'Today, euthanasia means deliberately terminating the life of another person by an act or omission in the context of terminal, painful or distressing illness.'

A failure by a doctor to provide a patient with treatment thought by responsible medical opinion to be necessary in the circumstances, could well be a criminal omission, whereas at the other end of the scale no doctor need resort to 'heroic methods' to prolong life.

Involuntary euthanasia: is ending the person's life without any indication on his or her part that he or she wished it to be so. This amounts to murder, even though the motive in ending that life may have been well-intended, *eg* the termination of suffering.

Voluntary euthanasia: is ending the person's life at their specific request. This category has been at the centre of attempts to legalise euthanasia. The 'specific request' is currently interpreted by supporters of the procedure, not only as a request at the time of the distressing illness, but also in advance, *eg* by means of a Living Will.

Non-voluntary euthanasia: is ending the life of a person who lacks the capacity either to know or to express his or her own wishes as to continued existence. Such a situation would arise in infants; in patients with severe brain damage or dementia; in severely mentally impaired people; and in the persistent vegetative state (PVS). The distinction between 'involuntary' and 'non-voluntary' is more than academic since the person in the former case would be capable of making a decision if given the opportunity. It is partic-ularly important to bear in mind the situation of infants and children in terminal or severe illness and handicap.

Much of the debate concerning euthanasia revolves around adults, notably the elderly and the younger adult with progressive illness, but the problems may arise just as acutely at the earlier stages of life. The law is, in fact, the same for every age.

2 Suicide: the taking of one's own life

While no change has occurred in the definition of suicide, it would appear that public condemnation of suicide as an act is less than in previous times. Suicide is still recognised by most people as a tragedy, but no longer as a sin. Any fear of judgement has been pushed into the background, and the concept of self-release has tended to take its place. This also may be related to change in the personal view of life and death and of one's responsibility for life, associated with a widespread rejection of Christian views and values. Even prior to 1961, when suicide ceased to be a crime in England, suicide was not criminal in Scotland, although before 1823 in Scotland suicides would not be buried in consecrated ground, and in some areas macabre rituals were associated with their burial.

Recent trends relating to suicide

A recent disturbing increase in suicide amongst younger men has been noted and various reasons suggested for this trend. Lower rates of marriage, higher divorce rates, high rates of unemployment, misuse of alcohol and drugs, the threat posed by AIDS and increased risk of imprisonment, have all been suggested as reasons. This trend has been noted in several countries, but the increase in the rates amongst men in the 15 to 24 age group was worse in the UK, when compared with those in most other countries in the European Community (*British Journal of Psychiatry:* Pritchard 160, 750-756). There is no convincing evidence of an increase in recognised mental illness associated with this trend, but it has been suggested that the treatment in the community of increasing numbers of people with mental illness may leave them more vulnerable, unless major support is available.

The position
of the Church of Scotland on suicide

The Church of Scotland's position on suicide remains clear. It offers compassion and understanding rather than condemnation.

3 Living Will (or Advance Directives)

A **Living Will** is a document in which the wishes of the person are defined in respect of the treatment which he or she may wish to receive, or not to receive, at some point in the future when they might be unable to give expression to these desires. This is a fairly recent concept, although it has been prevalent in the USA for a longer time. The **Advance Directives** Bill, introduced in the House of Lords, proposed similar provisions, together with the appointment of an agent to act for the person in the interpretation of their intentions, and there is some overlap with **Health-Care Proxy Documents** and the granting of a **Power of Attorney**. The distinctions between these may be quite subtle and are discussed to some extent later in this book.

What does the BIBLE say about EUTHANASIA?

Biblical and theological aspects

The Old and New Testaments do not specifically address many of our present day problems and questions related to 'letting someone die'. Scripture is probably silent because those problems didn't exist in Biblical times. The absence of respirators, drip therapies, heart pumps and feeding tubes did not confuse the difference between the process of dying and sustaining life.

'The Church of Scotland's position on suicide remains clear. It offers compassion and understanding rather than condemnation.'

So writes Joni Eareckson Tada from her personal perspective of having lived as a quadraplegic for some 25 years.

Scriptural principles

However, scripture does give us clear principles from which to draw our conclusions on this issue.

1 Man is God's creation

Scripture affirms that people owe their physical and spiritual existence to God alone, and that God must remain in control over their life. The 'I AM' God creates. Ultimate authority in matters of life and death rests solely with God from whom that life derives. It follows, then, that a Man's life is not his property: it is a loan. As such it must be held in trust. In the broadest sense it is meant for the service of God as suggested in the parable of the talents:

> *Again, it will be like a man going on a journey, who called his servants and entrusted his property to them. To one he gave five talents of money, to another two talents and to another one talent, each according to his ability.*
>
> (Matthew 25:14-15)

2 Man is made in the image of God

God chose to make His first revelation of His being and nature in the creation of Mankind, whom He chose to be His companion, His friend, and the expression of His purposes; One who might 'glorify Him and enjoy Him for ever'.

In creation, God has set humankind apart from 'the fish, the birds, and all the animals, domestic and wild, large and small' (Genesis 1:26) and has 'placed him over all creation', with the responsibility of stewardship for all the created order. We are therefore different from the rest of creation and we should recognise that difference in our treatment of, and relationships with, other people, as well as the rest of creation.

3 God became Man in Christ Jesus

The Incarnation is the most substantial argument for respect for life, our own and that of others. Christ Himself exalted the status of Humanity by taking human flesh and form (Philippians 2:7) and identifies with us in our infirmity. Christ declares also that His humanity is represented to us by those whom He identifies as His brothers – 'I was sick and you took care of me' (Matthew 25:26). Here Jesus the God-man does more than simply identify Himself with humanity. He *is* a man, subject to personal suffering. Human life is seen in the person of Jesus to be the matter about which God is earnestly concerned and we therefore must also be concerned about it.

4 We bear responsibility for others

One of the earliest breaches of Man's God-given responsibility lay in the murder of Abel, and the rejection of that responsibility is expressed in Cain's rhetorical question: 'Am I my brother's keeper?' It is clear that God expects of us just such a level of involvement.

Throughout the Bible the assertion is that human life is precious and holy and that all people, well or ill, are created in God's image and, bearing the stamp of their Creator, are equal before God and in His love.

Our individual human worth does not depend upon ability, gifts, or the quality of our life, but rather on our status as beings, made in God's image and likeness, and bearing the worth and value which He laid upon us when He 'so loved … that He gave His only begotten Son'. Those who handle their own life as a divine loan, redeemed by Christ's Sacrifice, will of necessity treat that life, and the lives of others, with respect. In the providence of God we

' … human life is precious and holy and all people, well or ill, are created in God's image.'

page 15

must recognise that there is a 'time to die' (Ecclesiastes 3:1-2*a*). It is not within the individual's authority to choose this time, any more than control is given over the time of birth. There may be in some circumstances a longing to die, a weariness to 'be with Christ which is far better'. For the Christian, death may be welcomed with a clearly positive dimension, for it is the prelude to resurrection. Paul, the Apostle, reminds us, 'As by Man came death, by Man came also the resurrection from the dead' (1 Corinthians 15:21) and, of himself, proclaims 'For me to live is Christ ... to die is gain' (Philippians 1:21). We therefore may accept the longing to die, to pass through into Life eternal, but we dare not presume to transform that longing into a 'right to die'.

God's love is all-embracing. He is present at our birth and at our death and it is His presence which gives ultimate meaning and purpose to both.

What does the LAW say about EUTHANASIA?

Legal and Parliamentary issues

The present legal position in Scotland, England and Wales

In attempting to understand the present position of the law on euthanasia, it is important to set out certain underlying principles. While these principles are clear in themselves, difficulties do arise in their application to particular cases and where the principles are in conflict with each other. As a result, the law in this area is far from being fixed and is being continually reviewed and amended.

Sanctity of life

The primary and fundamental principle is that of the sanctity of human life. This is a principle long recognised in all societies based on the Judaeo-Christian ethic. Similarly this applies in most other religious systems, including Islam and Hinduism. It is enshrined in Article 2 of the European Convention for the Protection of Human Rights and Fundamental Freedoms[3], and in Article 6 of the International Covenant of Civil and Political Rights (1966). Fundamental though it is, however, this is not an absolute principle in law. There are recognised exceptions: *eg* it may be lawful to take the life of another in self-defence. Where the principle is applicable, the law takes the view that causing the death of another with intent to do so is murder. Two elements are involved: (1) **a guilty act** *and* (2) **the necessary intent**.

As to the guilty act, the law draws a distinction between committing a positive act which causes death, and not carrying out an act which would have prevented death. In general, an omission to prevent death is not a guilty act and cannot give rise to a conviction for murder. But, where the accused was under a duty to the deceased to carry out the act which he omitted to do, such omission could be sufficient for the crime of either murder or culpable homicide, depending on the intention of the accused.

As to the question of intent, it is important to realise that the concern of the Courts lies in intention, and not motive. The motivation, for example, of a doctor injecting a known lethal dose of a drug into a patient could be humane and well-meaning, but that would be of no relevance if his sole intent was to terminate life.

Self-determination

A further fundamental principle underlying this area of law is that

---

3   Cmd 8969 (1953).

of self-determination: *eg* that respect must be given to a patient's own wishes by those charged with his treatment and care. Thus, if a patient of sound mind refuses, however unreasonably, to consent to treatment or care (even care by which his life would or might be prolonged), the doctors responsible for that person's care must give effect to those wishes, even though they do not consider it to be in his or her best interests to do so.[4]

This means that a patient of sound mind may refuse in advance to give his consent to certain treatment before he becomes unconscious or incapable of communicating it. Should a doctor, in spite of such refusal, proceed to give treatment which interferes with that patient's physical integrity, an assault will have been committed on the patient, and also a civil wrong. Such a refusal must be made by the patient while of sound mind and free from any pressure, and must apply to the situation that has in fact arisen. The individual's consent is subject to this exception – the full extent of which has not yet been determined by the law – that there are certain assaults upon another's person to which the consent of that person is no defence. To take an extreme but highly relevant example, it is no defence to a charge of murder that the victim, however ill or in whatever pain or distress, gave consent to being killed.

Problems relating to definition

The problem which arises with applying these principles and their exceptions to the field of euthanasia, is that there is such a wide variety of definitions and categories. Voluntary euthanasia has been defined above, and here the distinction in law can be crucial. Actively to bring another's life to an end, whether to avoid or to end suffering, even at that person's specific request, is not lawful. Similarly, aiding and abetting the suicide of another, remains an offence. The law recognises that there may arise a situation in which

4   Airedale NHS Trust vs Bland

the clinician concerned, taking into account the accepted, responsible, body of medical opinion and weighing up the relevant clinical factors (and in consultation with family or carers), may conclude that further treatment is futile and not, therefore, in the patient's best interests. In such a case the law would respect the decision made.

The doctors' dilemma

The question remains: how can the doctors know that, legally, they have got it right? In England, since the Bland case, application to the Family Division of the High Court for endorsement (or the reverse) would be wise, before putting such a decision on treatment into effect.

In Scotland, whereas it was common belief that the local Procurator Fiscal could give such guidance, the situation is in fact less clear. The Solicitor General for Scotland has ruled that Fiscals could give no safe assurances to doctors that they would *not* face criminal proceedings, if they decided to withdraw life support treatment. This does leave doctors with the choice, either of attempting to have the matter dealt with by the courts, with all the associated expense and delay, or of taking a risk, where they deem it right and justifiable, in the hope and expectation that their decision will be respected by the criminal authorities. This situation is quite unsatisfactory for doctors, patients and relatives, since it leaves an uncertainty which might lead to defensive medical practice. There would seem to be a case for the acceptance of a verifiable and defined clinical judgement by the doctors concerned, since life support in an otherwise inevitably fatal condition is recognisable as futile and inappropriate. This is not euthanasia in the current sense, since the intent is not specifically to kill the patient. In some cases, following the withdrawal of treatment, the patient may survive. It should be noted that the law does not require a doctor, who is caring for a patient, to prolong that patient's life by any available means regardless of the quality of that life. It requires him to treat the person by all accepted and appropriate means.

The doctor's discretion

The law allows the doctor, as a responsible professional, a degree of discretion, having regard to such factors as the expectation of benefit from the treatment proposed, the overall prognosis of the condition and the likelihood of future pain or other symptoms. This same principle applies in the so-called 'phenomenon of double effect', where the doctor acting in accordance with established medical practice is aware that the proposed treatment will have beneficial effects – for instance, in the relief of pain – but is also aware of the possibility that the patient's expectation of life may be shortened. The patient's subsequent death will be regarded in law as exclusively caused by the underlying disease. The doctor will have acted lawfully because his intention in administering the medication was not to cause the patient's death, but to relieve his symptoms.

The law takes the view that, whereas general guidelines require to be laid down by the Courts, day to day clinical decisions and treatment must belong with the doctor caring for the patient.

The right to refuse

From the above, it is clear that the patient's right to refuse any form of treatment is already established in law, and that written instructions to this end are already valid and would normally be respected in relation to an established clinical situation. But a request to terminate life cannot legally be met.

Living Will or Advance Directives

An Advance Directive, as noted above, is a document in which an individual lays down instructions as to health-care management and

' ... a request to terminate life cannot legally be met.'

treatment to be applied in the event of their incapacity to make such decisions or convey such instructions at the time of occurrence of the circumstances envisaged. In different states in the USA, there is some diversity of definition between 'Living Will' documents, 'Advance Directives' and 'Health-Care Proxy' documents, but the Voluntary Euthanasia Society (VES), in a careful study of the matter, perceives no need to impose such distinctions. They suggest that 'Living Will' is a concept sufficiently understood to be generally used.

The limitations of a Will

The popular view that a will is inviolable is not true, even in the case of a property will, and conditions which are contrary to established law or public policy cannot be enforced. This is certainly the case in the Living Will instance, since such a Will cannot insist that a doctor, or anyone else, should put the Will-maker to death.

What do doctors think about Living Wills?

The medical view, as expressed by the British Medical Association, is that a Living Will may be welcomed as an opening for the discussion of the difficult questions raised by terminal illness, and considerable use has been made of them in the context of AIDS care and counselling. Neither the BMA, nor the AIDS support agencies, the Terence Higgins Trust and Milestone House, nor the Association for Palliative Medicine, see any need for legislative change.

What is the VES view of the Living Will?

The VES, on the other hand, does wish to see legislation to make the provisions of a Living Will binding upon the medical staff involved. They see this as a first step towards fully legalising euthanasia and, for the same reason, they wish to see a Proxy document separately legislated for, as a separate deed from a Living Will. No Will can 'work' without the appointment of an executor. The appointment of a 'Health-Care Proxy' to be in effect the executor of the Living Will, would greatly assist the effectiveness of such a document.

At present, only the person making the Living Will has the right to enforce it, and he is, by definition *incapax* (incapable of making valid legal decisions). The VES-supported Medical Treatment (Advance Directives) Bill – now defunct – would have made failure to observe the provisions of a Living Will a statutory criminal offence with penalties defined for the doctor found guilty of such an offence. This raises the curious concept of the doctor being found not guilty of an offence if he kills the patient, but guilty if he fails to do so.

To give treatment against the expressed wishes of the patient, however, is already assault at common law, and there is therefore nothing to prevent the patient refusing in advance. The wisdom of restricting the judgement of the doctor responsible for care at this sensitive time of life is a matter which would require careful consideration. The style of Living Will published by the Voluntary Euthanasia Society of Scotland (VESS) proposes the appointment of a *tutor dative* (an agent appointed by the court) by the Court of Session, but this is a cumbersome and expensive procedure.

Why not use Power of Attorney?

A simpler procedure would be the further extension of the ordinary Scots Law on Power of Attorney. Such a Power of Attorney, notarially executed and countersigned at the Town Hall, is generally effective all over the World, and many of the American States use the same term. Powers could be granted to demand or refuse treatment in the light of the granter's stated wishes, but the decisions would be made at the relevant time by the Attorney who would have the benefit of current information. The Law Reform (Miscellaneous Provisions) (Scotland) Act 1990 extended the law to allow a Power of Attorney to remain in force during the mental

'To give treatment against the expressed wishes of the patient, however, is already assault at common law ...'

incapacity of the granter. This has proved a very simple and trouble free provision for elderly people in particular.

Summary

In brief, a Living Will is already possible, but cannot be certainly effective, because the person making it is unlikely to have foreseen exactly the situation in which it might be expected to have effect. The necessity of applying to the courts for a *tutor dative* to be appointed is inconvenient, but any appointment by the Will-maker of a Proxy, would fall as soon as the maker of the Will became *incapax* (incapable of making or communicating decisions). The extension of powers of attorney to cover health-care decisions would provide solutions to these difficulties; but, as Joni Eareckson Tada expresses it in *When is it right to die?*, 'It boils down to this: do you want to be represented by a piece of paper, or a person'?

What do the POLITICIANS say about EUTHANASIA?

Recent Parliamentary developments

UK Parliament

Over the past few years there have been several attempts to introduce legislation on various aspects of medical decisions at the end of life. In May 1990 a Voluntary Euthanasia Bill was proposed in the Lower House by Mr Boyes MP, who had prepared the way by setting down an Early Day motion supported by 28 MPs. Thirty-five MPs voted for the Bill, 101 against it and 510 abstained. In February 1993, the Termination of Medical Treatment Bill was introduced in the House of Lords where it fell for lack of time. However, it is clear that a large proportion of our elected representatives remain to be convinced either way in this debate, and there is therefore a real possibility that a few very keen proponents of euthanasia could force through a measure when the majority are simply not present.

Although it did not explicitly refer to euthanasia, the Medical Treatment (Advance Directives) Bill, lost at the dissolution of the last Parliament, was seen and publicised by its supporters, the Voluntary Euthanasia Society, as a first step in that direction, and it will doubtless re-appear in the lifetime of this Parliament.

The European dimension

Since the Westminster Parliament is no longer our only source of legislation, we require also to consider developments in the European Community. There have been several moves, particularly by the Dutch, to persuade the rest of the Community to follow them in this field. Three approaches have been used to apply such pressure:

1   Media exposure of the 'benefits' of euthanasia.
2   Encouragements to the European Parliament to move into a field of new health law.
3   Raising discussions within the Council of Europe with the aim of achieving the establishment of a 'Commission on the Rights of the Dying'.[5]

So far these have been so successful that in September 1991, the EC Human Rights Commission stated: '*Wherever a sick person in perfect clarity of mind demands strongly and persistently that an end be put to an existence which has lost all meaning for him, and*

---

5   Dutch MP, Mr Kohnstamm and Euro MP I van der Heuvel at the 9th World Congress of Right to Die Societies: Maastricht, June 1990.

where a committee of doctors convoked for the purpose recognises the unavailability of any other treatment, euthanasia should be granted.'

Observation of clinical practice in the Netherlands suggests this is capable of being interpreted as, 'When one request has been made and there has been the briefest, undocumented discussion with one other doctor'.

These matters have been debated in the European Parliament, but have not been carried. It may be that a sufficient representation from Greece and Ireland has ensured effective opposition, but this situation may change when the Eastern European countries join.

EUTHANASIA
in the NETHERLANDS

Since the early 1970s euthanasia has been practiced in the Netherlands. It has become part of the accepted pattern of Medical practice and in a very real sense this allows us to examine the effect which liberalisation of the law in this respect may have.

There is a good deal of confusion as to the actual situation in Holland, not least because the law has taken a number of rather unusual turns and has only recently been clarified.

Under a new Dutch law passed in the early weeks of December 1993, euthanasia remains a criminal act punishable by up to 12 years in prison. The law simply gives a legal basis to the current procedure whereby doctors report euthanasia to the local coroner. The legal procedure requires the completion of a form which affirms and indicates that the following criteria have been met. This virtually guarantees them immunity from prosecution.

'Under a new Dutch law passed in the early weeks of December 1993, euthanasia remains a criminal act punishable by up to 12 years in prison.'

Criteria and procedure
for euthanasia in the Netherlands

1   *The request must come only from the patient and must be entirely free and voluntary.*

2   *The patient's request must be well considered, durable and persistent.*

3   *The patient must be experiencing intolerable, not necessarily physical, suffering.*

4   *Euthanasia must be a last resort. Other alternatives to alleviate the patient's situation must have been considered and found wanting.*

5   *Euthanasia must be performed by a physician.*

6   *The physician must consult with an independent physician colleague who has experience in the field.*

The form is submitted to the local coroner. The coroner notifies the public prosecutor of the doctor's report and the cause of death, and the public prosecutor's assessment of the case determines whether further proceedings should follow.

The previous situation

Prior to this form of regulation, 'necessity' was seen as a defence to the act of euthanasia if the appropriate steps were taken, but it was not a defence for giving a false death certificate. Despite this, a report[6] of the Royal Dutch Medical Association (KNMG) noted it was 'not unusual' for euthanasia to be reported as a natural death. The criteria stated above were in place in 1989, well before the recent acts of the Dutch Parliament, and might have been expected to provide careful and reasonable guidelines for the regulation of any clinical procedure carrying such grave and lasting implications, but observation of practice reveals that they did not in fact achieve their purpose.

---

6   'Vision on Euthanasia' 39, *Medish Contant* 990 (1984).

' … a report of the Royal Dutch Medical Association noted that it was "not unusual" for euthanasia to be reported as a natural death.'

The Remmelink Report

In September 1991 a Dutch Government committee, chaired by Attorney General Remmelink[7], reported that in 1990 there were 2000 deaths specifically recognised as euthanasia, and 400 cases of assisted suicide. One thousand people had their lives terminated without any specific request. 15,975 cases were reported in which the doctors concerned acknowledged that it was their explicit or secondary intention to shorten life by the administration of analgesic drugs (8100 cases) or by withdrawing or withholding treatment. A survey, also carried out in 1990, by Dutch Medical Examiner Van der Wal[8] and others, revealed that in 13% of cases the interval between the first request for euthanasia and its performance was no more than 1 day. In 35% it was no more than 1 week, and in a further 17% it was no more than 2 weeks. The interval between the last request for euthanasia and its performance was no more than 1 day in 3 out of 5 cases, and in 22% of cases the interval between the first and the last request was between 1 hour and 1 week. In almost two thirds of cases the request was purely oral, and the requirement for a second opinion has been called in question by one of the Dutch public prosecutors. It has been estimated that some 70% of cases were never reported to the competent authority, and out of 50,000 deaths in Holland which involved medical opinion, 20,000 had either direct or indirect, voluntary or involuntary euthanasia applied.[9]

' ... out of 50,000 deaths in Holland which involved medical opinion, 20,000 had either direct or indirect, voluntary or involuntary euthanasia applied.'

The doctor's conscience

In the Netherlands, even with the revision of the law which defines clear guidelines and practical legal procedures, the practice of killing people where cure is not likely ultimately remains open to the

---

7   Remmelink Report (1991).
8   Remmelink Report (1991).
9   J Keown: Euthanasia Conference, Strathclyde University (24 April 1993).

individual doctor, whose only real sanction is his or her own conscience. A doctor working in Holland is reported as commenting, 'It is difficult the first time you do it, but it gets easier with experience', and this comment fits well with our experience of human nature. The same comment was made recently by a young offender who was interviewed on radio about his record of stealing cars!

The consequences of legalised euthanasia

The development of palliative medicine in the Netherlands is relatively limited and Hospice provision is minimal. The response to this, by those supporting this system, is to indicate that home care facilities for the treatment of terminal illness are better developed and that comprehensive health-care provisions cover the need.

A report of the Health Council on Palliative Care in the Netherlands, however, concluded that 54% of cancer patients who were in pain, suffered unnecessarily because doctors and nurses had insufficient understanding of the nature of the pain and the possibilities for its alleviation.[10] A handbook on palliative care was subsequently issued by the Council to all Dutch doctors.

The Dutch situation is held out as a desirable one by the supporters of euthanasia who would wish to see the same 'liberal and enlightened' legislation in the UK. The dangers are not difficult to perceive. Writing in 1806, Christoph Hufeland stated:

> The physician should and may do nothing else but preserve life. Whether it is valuable or not, that is none of his business. If he once permits such considerations to influence his actions, the doctor will become the most dangerous person in the state.

The current situation in the Netherlands suggests that these words are as valid today as they have ever been.

---

10   'The Law and Practice of Euthanasia in The Netherlands' in *Ethics and Medicine:* J Keown (1992), 8.3, 34-48.

MEDICAL ISSUES *in* EUTHANASIA, SUICIDE *and* LIVING WILLS

The whole area of the management of the terminal phase of illness and the end of life is one in which medical practice is, of necessity, deeply involved. The manner in which the patient dies, whether in acute illness or in longer term chronic illness, may even be something of a touchstone for the quality of medical care. Since the dawn of the profession, doctors have been involved with dying; relieving its distresses, seeking to support the patient in the process, whether long or short.

Acceptance of death

One of the most difficult disciplines for the physician or surgeon, is to come to terms with the ultimate failure of all the therapeutic measures available to them and with which they have practiced. Death may be postponed, even avoided, but not ultimately evaded. If it is difficult for the doctor to countenance death, seeing it as the ultimate failure of art and skill, it would be even more difficult for the doctor to see him or herself as the personal agent of that failure. The wise and experienced doctor will certainly seek to use the skills of medicine to alleviate the pains and distresses of death, and indeed to make the process of dying as free of distress as possible for the terminally ill person.

'Death may be postponed, even avoided, but not ultimately evaded.'

Suicide

Suicide, although not an offence in law, remains offensive to most doctors. It is perceived among the most negative of emergencies to be handled in the casualty and intensive care areas of general hospitals and, while compassion and understanding are readily

'Suicide, although not an offence in law, remains offensive to most doctors.'

extended to the unsuccessful victim, that sympathy and under-standing are directed towards the person, rather than towards the act. The suicide of a patient who has been under regular care, whether terminally ill, psychiatrically depressed or in severe distress for other reasons, is a particular trauma to most health care professionals who may carry, in addition to the sense of failure when the patient dies, an equally distressing feeling that in some way they have failed that person while they were still alive and still amenable to supportive help.

Assisted suicide

Assisted suicide is seen, with justification, as the first step towards euthanasia. It is suggested by the supporters of euthanasia that both doctors and carers are regularly dealing with the intractable symptoms of seriously or terminally ill patients in this way, making available the means of self-destruction, but allowing the person concerned to take the definitive action which is required to end life. They call for an end to the 'hypocrisy' of this approach.

However, it is striking that in many instances of distressing and painful illness, a supply of medication which would be entirely sufficient to end life is left in the full control of the patient with instructions for safe self-medication and in only a few cases is this trust manifestly abused. Nor is it often abused when such instructions are given to the principal carer. It is doubtful whether the legal sanction by itself is enough to totally inhibit such action, but legalisation of physician assisted suicide would carry the same problems as the legalisation of euthanasia of any nature – it would loosen the ethical basis of much medical practice.

Legalisation of a defence of assisted suicide by relatives, carers or anyone else would be even more unsafe and would expose the caring situation to even greater pressures of a very serious nature.

Suicide and assisted suicide are neither a safe, nor a satisfactory, answer to the relief of distressing illness.

'Suicide and assisted suicide are neither a safe, nor a satisfactory, answer to the relief of distressing illness.'

Those who do promote such legalisation make much of the anomaly that, while suicide itself has been decriminalised, assisting suicide remains a criminal act. While it may be possible to interpret the intent of the suicide – him or herself – in the light of illness or psychological disturbance, such extenuating arguments cannot be applied to the person who assists. The motivation of compassion may be claimed, but many other factors may also be playing a part, and the safeguards of the law remain appropriate.

Over the years the Medical and Nursing professions have steadfastly set their faces against such a change in the law, and with a few vociferous exceptions, doctors and nurses feel that they neither need it nor want it. Why should this be?

The ethos of medical practice

It is no part of the doctor's tradition or ethos to kill. This option was open in pre-Hippocratic Medicine, but Hippocratic tradition, and later, Judaeo-Christian teaching, set out to change this and to oblige the doctor to preserve and sustain life by every means possible. It has always been accepted that death could not be postponed indefinitely, but the duty of the doctor as expressed by Ambroise Pare 'to cure sometimes, to alleviate often, to comfort always', has stopped short of death as a treatment option. There is still in most doctors an abhorrence of killing, even accidentally, and a deeper abhorrence of doing so intentionally.

'There is still in most doctors, an abhorrence of killing, even accidentally, and a deeper abhorrence of doing so intentionally.'

Advances in treatment

The treatment of illness and the relief of suffering have advanced very considerably in the past three decades. Much of what was previously incurable is being effectively treated, what was intractable is finding relief, and what was chronically disabling is now often responsive to rehabilitative measures. We can do a great deal more than we ever could previously.

On the other side of the coin, however, there is still a great deal which cannot be remedied and increased longevity is now presenting us with the problems of the illnesses of later life.

Symptom control has also made major advances. Pain relief is more effective than at any time in human history. Our understanding of the nature of pain and human responses to it are increasing steadily. Pharmacological and physical methods for its relief are available and effective for conditions and circumstances which would have been previously resistant. Drug delivery systems, special formulations, chemotherapeutic agents, physical techniques such as TENS (Transcutaneous Electrical Nerve Stimulation) are pushing back the thresholds of pain and bringing relief to those who are appropriately assessed and treated. Often the problem is that the individual patient, in terminal or distressing illness, may be less well treated than they ought to be, because the individual doctor is less well informed or equipped than he or she should be. Emphasis is placed in debate on the very small number of people whose pain cannot be relieved, but much more frequent is the situation of the person whose pain might have been relieved, but has not.

The attractions of the easy way out

If there is a less demanding alternative open to doctors, it is more likely to be chosen than the more demanding, if it is legal or if it can be justified. Most doctors who have to deal with the very ill and terminally ill will admit to having been tempted at some time to bring a patient's life to an end, and no doubt some have yielded to that temptation. But temptation with opportunity and without sanction becomes licence: the doctor should not be licensed to kill.

A group of Dutch doctors was asked if they had ever carried out euthanasia or assisted suicide: 54% said 'yes'. The others were asked if they would, if asked to do so: 34% said 'yes'. Those who said 'no' were asked if they would refer their patients to others

'Pain relief is more effective than at any time in human history.'

' … temptation with opportunity and without sanction becomes licence: the doctor should not be licensed to kill.'

who would do so: 8% said they would. Only 4% said they would never carry out euthanasia.

These observations reinforce the concern that legalisation of euthanasia would change medical practice and would bring about a significant change in public perception of illness and of the doctor. The Law enshrines what is socially acceptable, and unless doctors have strong moral or religious objections, they will tend to do what they know to be socially acceptable. In practice, those who strongly oppose such a principle will not carry out the procedure, and may even exclude themselves from the practice of the relevant specialty. Those who are in favour of the principle will do it with conviction.

The majority, accepting what is required of them, are prepared to get on with it without a great deal of thought about it. Among these are many who, had they been asked, would have declared themselves against it before the law changed, but will rationalise their change of attitude.

Compassion need not kill

The compassionate motivation of those who support euthanasia is not in dispute, but it is unsafe to encourage or even to allow compassion to perceive death as its only or prime instrument. There is already concern that physicians in the Netherlands consider this option much more readily than before, apparently to the exclusion of valid alternatives.

What are the practical problems?

There are several practical problems to be considered in the legalisation of euthanasia, and several questions to be asked. These tend to be discounted by the proponents as being much over-rated, and grounds for only secondary objection.

1 How voluntary is the decision?

Many influences bear upon us in illness. Depressive illness distorts our judgement. The doctor's approach, the family's desires, financial matters, the feeling of being unwanted and being a burden – all of these demonstrably influence the older person in particular in the less radical decisions which they have to make in late life. Would they not also influence their decision about euthanasia?

2 What controls would there be on the practice, and how would they be regulated?

The drawing up of regulations under which euthanasia might be practised is an academic exercise, unless these regulations can be monitored more closely than seems to be current experience with such regulations elsewhere.

3 What measures of diagnostic integrity should be established?

A post-mortem examination would need to be obligatory to confirm pre-mortem diagnosis. This safeguard has never appeared in any of the proposals set forward. And what redress is proposed if the doctor has got it wrong? Equally, what does the doctor do about his own feelings of guilt if he *does* get it wrong?

4 What conditions should qualify?

For instance, the currently intractable today, which may be treatable tomorrow? Or conditions which might be expected to get worse – and how much worse? Perhaps all conditions which cause severe distress? Would this include clinical depression in which the patient as a part of the illness simply wants to die? (Such a case has been brought to the Dutch legal authorities.) Should we then abandon the treatment of all attempted suicides?

Diagnostic and prognostic uncertainties are, in themselves, a challenge to medical advance in research, in diagnosis, in treatment and in symptom relief. Take away the challenge and we might stop trying!

5 Would euthanasia address the real fears of most people?

It is not usually death itself that people fear, it is the process of dying, and the possibility of being subjected to unpleasant treatment with no real purpose except that of satisfying a hypothetical concept of medical science. What most people want and need is the reassurance that relief will be given, and that there is no medical 'hidden purpose' in their management. Given that reassurance, fear departs and the desire for euthanasia quickly evaporates.

Hospice doctors, involved constantly in symptom relief for the terminally ill, testify consistently that the relief of symptoms with the confidence that this relief will be made readily available, effectively disposes of the request for death.

Where symptoms are properly controlled, death again becomes unattractive.

Fear of 'meddlesome medicine'

It should be noted that meddlesome interventionist medicine is as abhorrent to a doctor committed to good terminal care as it is to the most active supporter of euthanasia, and it is as morally reprehensible to leave a patient in a state of suffering without relief as it is to kill them. However, it is equally unnecessary to do either. Legalising euthanasia would increase pressure on the vulnerable and would be used for reversible pain.

A euthanasia mentality

There is a real danger that a 'euthanasia mentality', which does not even consider the alternatives when faced with terminal illness, may develop. A paper presented recently by a doctor with experience of the Dutch situation[11], suggested that this indeed was becoming established in Holland where many people were beginning to see euthanasia as a right, in the event of developing a terminal illness.[12]

Summary

Doctors, with a few exceptions, are not in the forefront of the demand for euthanasia and would view it as unnecessary. They are, however, involved in the ethical and moral debate around the issues of terminal care.

Technical advance has brought its dilemmas which require to be considered carefully and responsibly against an ethical background, but it has also brought much improved potential for relief of the distresses of illness.

Legal involvement has not proved generally helpful and previous legal rulings have tended to pass the specific issues back to the doctors concerned. The basic need is for better clinical awareness of the principles of good management of troublesome symptoms and, as a consequence, better education and training of health-care professionals in these principles. Good clinical judgement is based on knowledge, compassion and integrity. Were the law on euthanasia changed, this would seriously alter the role and perception of the public and the profession, and would increase rather than decrease the pressures and anxieties which are currently expressed in the context of medical decisions at the end of life.

11   Dr Helen Sweeney: Conference on the Ethics of Euthanasia from a Judaeo-Christian point of view in London (16 November 1993).
12   ibid.

Euthanasia in childhood and infancy

In the practice of Paediatric Medicine there are two main areas in which euthanasia may be relevant – Paediatric terminal illness and Neonatal intensive care.

Paediatric terminal illness

The conscious child

Most conscious children requiring terminal care are cancer patients, but some have meningitis or other progressive conditions. Palliative care for these has recently received new emphasis, as expansion in the field with specialised Hospice provision for children has occurred.

By contrast, in Holland, where the euthanasia concept is widely accepted, there is no such specialist provision. Euthanasia is overtly perceived as the solution to these problems.

The emotional aspects of caring for a dying child are difficult for parents and for staff to handle, irrespective of the symptoms of the condition. Carers must consider the autonomy of children, as well as considering them as people who do have a right and a need to know what is happening to them in terms which they can understand. A child, like an adult, has the right to have wishes, feelings and preferences, and to express them; and this must include the opportunity to accept or refuse treatment: *eg* further chemotherapy where there may be doubt as to the likelihood of response.

It is responsible and necessary to give factual information to a child as much as to an adult, and experience has shown that children may handle the terminal care situation better than many adults.

'A child … has the right to have wishes, feelings and preferences, and to express them, and … the opportunity to accept or refuse treatment.'

Family involvement, which includes siblings in decisions, results in easier relationships and management of difficult situations. Counselling of a whole family is often necessary and involvement of other children in family grief has a healing effect. Long family silence about a dead child is found to be common, and in general has a destructive effect.

Adequate symptom relief, sometimes self-administered and controlled by the child (who can become very skilled at it), and support for the family through the time of trauma, result in the elimination of the need for intentional killing.

The demand for euthanasia for children

There is no demand from parents for intentional killing and the matter is raised more by ethicists and theoreticians than by anyone in the practical field. The majority of paediatricians are against intentional killing and medically assisted suicide, but there is a small group who would support its introduction.

One report indicates that children have been supplied with a lethal injection and have been encouraged to administer this to themselves 'when all else has failed'. In such a situation, you wonder whether compassion and care had indeed failed the child!

Unconscious children

These are usually sufferers from trauma, head injury, and brain lesions of various kinds. The most frequent problem encountered is head injury related to traffic accidents. They have often been dealt with in adult intensive care units until recently, when paediatric units have been opened. The criteria for brainstem death are the same as in adults. Similar debates occur over brainstem death in children as in adult cases. 'Switch-off' decisions are generally made on the same grounds of negative expectation of recovery, but practice varies.

The parents have the veto and often wish to continue life support initially, but may reach a point of acceptance of the futility of this after an opportunity to come to terms with the realities of the situation. Improved resuscitation techniques have really introduced these problems, since many would have died without these being applied.

Where the life-support requires to be switched off, this is usually done with the parents present, one of them holding the child in the period after switch-off.

The normal expectation is that death will occur. However, the expectation of death may not always be fulfilled, and a brain damaged child requiring a major level of support remains. In one incident, following which the child was later fostered in a loving home where care is excellent, major guilt still produces problems for the parents. The case for euthanasia in such cases would rest more upon the suffering of the parents rather than that of the child.

Neonatal care

The specialist field of neonatology came into being to meet the needs of infants delivered in difficult midwifery situations. Low birth weight (premature) children – less than 3.5lbs – account for about 1% of births, and survival for such children before specialist intervention occurred was about 25%. This is now around 75%.

Malformed children account for about 1–2% of all births and, with the important exception of brain malformations, the prognosis for normal life for many of these children is fairly good as neonatal intensive care and surgery have improved. Many previously lethal malformations are treatable with good outcome if diagnosis is made early, and detection techniques are improving so that early treatment is made possible.

Professional attitudes to this type of work are ambivalent. Some consider these infants as 'nature's duds' and would not feel that any treatment was appropriate, especially in view of the high costs

'Many previously lethal malformations are treatable with good outcome if diagnosis is made early.'

page 39

involved. 'Foetal Medicine' – concerned mainly with screening for abnormality and termination of pregnancy, if such abnormality is found – has been developing in parallel.

In this context it is permissible both in Scots Law, and more recently in English Law, to terminate a pregnancy for reasons of severe foetal abnormality right up to term.

Parental instinct and personhood

It has been observed that, in deciding how much should be done in such cases of malformation and birth abnormality, a good deal of reliance may be placed upon the intuitive responses of parents and others involved, since the general philosophy is still towards the concept of sanctity of life. This may owe something to the general awareness of a Judaeo-Christian heritage and background.

In some areas of secular philosophy, however, opinions may differ very markedly from this approach. Some would express the idea that a child is not yet fully a person, but only a *potential* person, and therefore should have no rights until it has self-awareness. This view is reminiscent of the arguments about personhood in the abortion debate. It is striking that ethicists seem to differ quite markedly from the general public in these matters!

The factors in change in paediatrics

Five general changes were noted as influencing practice in children:

1 **Technical advances**, making things possible which could not happen before – often bringing problems as well as advantages.

2 The possibility of **assigning prognosis** to conditions found by screening raises the problem of information being available

which it may not be appropriate or helpful to possess (*eg* a bad prognosis given ante-natally, which is not fulfilled post-natally may have a negative effect upon parental attitude towards the child). This is important because a high rate of false positive results is encountered in screening procedures. Unless action is to be taken on the results of screening – *eg* termination of pregnancy – the screening may be counter-productive.

3   The **new consumerism** has an effect upon attitudes when things go wrong with the neonate. Society, as well as the individual, are seeking control of life's events; technology seems to offer this, including control of the arrival of children on time and perfect. A baby may be viewed as a 'consumer product' or accession and biological variation may not be acceptable: a view which leads readily to the attitude – 'if it is not right, dispose of it'.

From the Christian perspective, GOD has control – we do not. Our lives are in God's hands at the beginning and the end. Human goal setting, ambition and consumerism must give way to our accountability and stewardship of life and relationships, for which we are answerable to God Himself. The question, 'Am I my brother's keeper?', still evokes the answer 'yes!' from the highest authority in the matter.

4   **Secular philosophy** – discussed above – proposes the idea that babies are potential people, not real people. They are capable of life to the full, but if they are seen as not 'capable', they are likely to be considered disposable.

5   **Health-care economics**. Pressure on resources requires allocation of priorities. Babies may not be seen as a priority, especially if deformed or abnormal! Economics asks the question, ' Is this expense good value for money?'

The Christian response

The Christian response will involve:

1   Palliative Care with response and resources and higher motivation.
2   Better communication in respect of the child, taking account of the need for counselling and a recognition and respect for the child, equally, as a person formed in the image of God.
3   Valid motivation: the phrase 'compassion mingled with respect', attributed to Mother Teresa, perhaps sums up the most constructive attitude and is very much in keeping with the spirit of the Lord's words – 'In as much as ye did it unto one of the the least of these, my brothers, ye did it unto me' (Matthew 25:40). The irreducible minimum of care was defined as – fluid and nutrition, analgesia and tender loving care (TLC). If a community is to claim to be civilised, it must care for its disadvantaged.

What does SOCIETY have to say about EUTHANASIA?

Sociological issues and pressure groups

The Board's report *Family Matters*, published in 1992, makes reference to rapid changes in the structure of family life in Britain over the past thirty years. Divorce, separation and marriage breakdown are more prevalent than at any time in the past. Mobility of families, with separation of younger members to go to other parts of the country, or even abroad, for reasons of employment, and the increased pressure for both partners to work, have all decreased the cohesion of the community. These factors also weaken the caring infra-structure of society. The number of households of only one person, often an older person, has increased, and the threads of relationship with which the fabric of care is woven, are weakened.

It is striking that 'Community Care' is now an officially established statutory organisation, rather than the spontaneous response of the looser community to the need for care for its more dependent members. Dependent people – be they old, ill, or disabled – can readily feel forgotten, or may come to see themselves as a burden to their busy, mobile families. They may indeed be perceived as a burden by these families, by neighbours, or by society itself, and once that perception is established, society and individuals begin to explore the means to get rid of the burden, rather than to solve the individual problems. This is the context of pressure for euthanasia.

'Dependent people, – be they old, ill, or disabled – can readily feel forgotten, or may come to see themselves as a burden to their busy, mobile families.'

Health-care expectations

As the expectation of relief of illness and health improvement in response to improved medical care and technology increases, so the acceptability of progressive, distressing or painful illness becomes less, and the demand increases for an 'easy way out'. At the same time the demand for autonomy and control has increased with wider awareness of health-care issues, and the previous style of paternalistic medical care is less acceptable.

Quality of life

The 'quality of life' is an issue frequently introduced to the euthanasia debate. Measurement of the effects of various therapeutic procedures is attempted using 'Quality Adjusted Life Years' (QALYs) which seek to answer: 'What quality of life will it give for how long?' Quality of life is often assessed on a purely hedonistic basis, the question being – 'How much happiness is a person in this situation able to experience?'; whereas a Christian view would measure such quality in terms of relationship – with God and with others.

The doctor is required to deliver such 'quality', as well as treatment of illness as it may arise. Expectation of medical intervention, often quite legitimately, to manipulate non-disease related problems has also increased. Contraception, termination of pregnancy, tranquillisers for performance demands, and hormone replacement therapy, are requested for reasons often quite unrelated to illness or the threat of it, and the demand for the manipulation of the end of life may be seen as a logical further step.

Pressure groups

1 The Appleton conference

The Appleton Conference Project began with an international working conference for practising clinicians regarding decisions to withhold or withdraw life-sustaining treatments. In 1991 the responses were summarised in a report: 'The Appleton International Conference – developing guidelines for decisions to forego life-prolonging medical treatment'. This document underlines four *prima facie* moral principles:

1 **Autonomy**
   All persons have a moral obligation to respect each other's autonomy.
2 **Non-maleficence**
   All persons have a moral obligation not to harm each other.
3 **Beneficence**
   All persons have a moral obligation to benefit others.
4 **Justice**
   All persons have a moral obligation to act justly or fairly to others.

Acknowledgement of these principles provide a valuable cross-cultural basis for medical moral analysis, discussions and decision-making. The first group considered are those who have a decision-making capacity, or who have provided oral or written advanced directives before losing that capacity. Three groups of patients are identifiable within this category:

1   Those who refuse treatment.
2   Those who request treatment, including life-prolonging treatment which may be considered futile.
3   Those who may request intervention intended to terminate life.

Where a patient had previously given an advance directive in any of these areas, doctors were considered to have a strong moral obligation to respect such requests.

The second group considered was those who have lost the capacity to make decisions and who have not executed an advance directive. The guidelines recognise two choices:

1   To forego rather than to use a particular treatment; *or*
2   To decide, from several possible alternatives, which treatment should be used.

Factors influencing these decisions will include the doctor's clinical responsibility and the possible conflict of views of care-givers or family members. A particular weight of responsibility falls upon doctors caring for socially isolated patients and those diagnosed as being in a persistent vegetative state (PVS).

The third group identified was that of patients who currently lack, and have always lacked, the capacity for choice for themselves of life-prolonging treatment. In these cases, no 'substituted judgement' can be made, since their wishes and desires cannot be known. Third person judgements about quality of life are inevitable in setting reasonable limits for treatment in these circumstances, and, where the patient lacks a surrogate, decisions will depend upon a weighing of the benefits and burdens.

Dissent

In the Conference itself, dissent to the guideline on euthanasia was expressed by a number of participants on the grounds that, understandable though such a request might be, it is not morally justified and that statutory legislation for the intentional killing of patients by doctors is contrary to basic morality.

Dissenting from the guidelines on PVS, some members could not accept a categorical exclusion of the use of life sustaining treatments, especially hydration and nutrition.

Conditions of scarcity

The Conference also considered guidelines on decisions to forego life sustaining treatments under conditions of scarcity.

These involve an understanding of the ethical demands of justice and efficiency, and the conflicts which may arise between these and the demands of autonomy and beneficence, in conditions of scarcity.

It remains the duty of the doctor to offer all that is of benefit to his patient, unless it is otherwise prescribed by society, decisions being imposed upon doctors at a clinical level by some measure of legal force. A decision prescribed by society should not be disguised as a medical decision.

'A decision prescribed by society should not be disguised as a medical decision.'

2 The Voluntary Euthanasia Societies

The Voluntary Euthanasia Societies (VES) were significantly less aggressive than the views expressed in the 'Right to Die Societies' Conferences would hold, and a strong emphasis is laid upon the 'Voluntary' aspect of their aims.

There is common ground between them and those who oppose euthanasia', in so far as the persistence of pain or distress in terminal illness is seen as abhorrent, and the motivation of compassion is readily recognised.

Much emphasis is laid upon the concept of autonomy, with which agreement was also possible, but the problems of implementation were much less readily accepted. It does not seem credible to the VES that the autonomy of other, vulnerable, people might be put in jeopardy by the kind of changes which the Society envisages, nor does it seem to be apparent to them the extent to which such legislation might alter the ethos and relationships of medical practice.

A beneficent provision?

Euthanasia is perceived as an entirely charitable provision from which suffering Mankind can only benefit. Suggestions that abuse is not only possible, but demonstrable, in the Dutch experience, as well as in the earlier part of the present century, were dismissed as either exaggerated or irrelevant.

The view seemed to be that for a significant proportion of dying people, compassion can only be expressed by a willingness to end the suffering by intentionally killing the patient, and much of the experience of the Hospice Movement very effectively rebuts this view.

Euphemisms

Although the word 'euthanasia' is retained in the title of the Societies, alternative phrases are often used to avoid emotive distortion and to seek consensus. The use of such euphemisms leads to confusion – as in the gradation of physician-assisted suicide, physician aid in dying and 'do not resuscitate' orders – and there is considerable concern over the grey area between active voluntary euthanasia and involuntary euthanasia.

Symptom control

The VES does not accept that pain control is as achievable as the experience of Hospice staff has shown it to be, nor do they accept that the demand for euthanasia is abandoned when adequate symptom control is established.

It is unfortunate also that the VES perpetuates the false notion that drugs used to relieve pain invariably pose the dilemma of the so-called 'double effect', *ie* that adequate dosage to relieve pain must inevitably shorten life. This myth has led to much unnecessary suffering by patients who refuse pain-relieving drugs under the misapprehension that these will inevitably hasten death.

Many doctors in the fields of terminal and palliative care will testify that the effect of symptom relief – using drugs such as the opiates which are reputed to have such a 'double effect' hazard – quite often is to extend the patient's life by relief of debilitating and exhausting symptoms.

Opiate abuse unquestionably shortens life in the context of the illegal drugs scene, but their correct use, even in high dosage, does not shorten the life of the patient with malignant pain.

ALTERNATIVES *to the* PROGRESSION *of* EUTHANASIA?

Hospice care and palliative medicine

Development and principles

Over the past three decades the Hospice Movement has led the way in improving the care of dying patients. This improvement has been achieved, not only by in-patient units, but also, and more extensively, by the community palliative care services provided by

Macmillan Nurses and Marie Curie Nursing staff. The underlying philosophy of the movement has been the recognition of the importance of quality of life involving physical, emotional, psycho-social, intellectual and spiritual aspects of that quality.

Much of the development has been towards patients with advanced cancer, but the principles are just as applicable to other conditions and the benefits should be available to all. Palliative care has tended to be sought by hospital as well as general practitioners, as a last resort, towards the end of the course of an illness, but there is much to be said for earlier referral. The skills of palliative care require to be applied as an integral part of the management of the condition and should be considered much more often and applied at an earlier time if the greatest benefit in terms of quality of life is to be obtained.

Multi-disciplinary caring

An integrated approach to the patient's problems is achieved best by a multi-disciplinary team which will involve medical, nursing, paramedical and other professional personnel, and the input of the Church is by no means irrelevant in this context. The Hospital Chaplain or minister may be an extremely important member of the team.

Standards of care

The principal challenge is to duplicate the high standards of patient care and symptom relief as established in the field of cancer care, to influence the approach to the terminal stages of many other diseases.

Pain relief and symptom control

Pain relief is a major issue in the quality of life. In cancer care pain is often seen by the lay public as one of the primary symptoms. In

'Pain relief is a
major issue in the
quality of life.'

fact 25% of cancer patients never suffer pain, and of those who do, some 10% to 15% have severe pain. In 98% of patients this severe pain can be controlled without undue sedation, and even where pain is resistant it can be considerably reduced. Non-malignant pain, on the other hand, is very debilitating, very destructive and has proved more difficult to control.

Such pain, often continuing for years, may have a psychological as well as a physical component and may be compounded by anxiety and depression. Methods of pain control have improved even in this area and Pain Control clinics, while patchy in availability, are making advances in methods and approaches to persistent pain.

Who asks for euthanasia and why?

'There is increasing
evidence that
requests for
euthanasia come
from patients whose
symptom control
has been less than
adequate.'

There is increasing evidence that requests for euthanasia come from patients whose symptom control has been less than adequate, and these requests are very rarely sustained after good symptom control has been established. Often the demand arises out of fear of unbearable suffering. When it becomes apparent that this fear is unfounded and that relief will be available, the fear itself is allayed and the apparent need for euthanasia is diminished.

Availability of care

The argument, sometimes presented for euthanasia, that good palliative care is not generally available, does not hold up in face of the facts. Very few Health Boards and Authorities remain without a specialist palliative care service and research is still expanding into all aspects of symptom control.

As noted above, the demand for euthanasia in the Netherlands is associated with less development of palliative care. In 1992 in Holland, there were no Palliative Care/Hospice services, although five such Units were planned. This compares with the UK where there were 183 in-patient Hospices already established, some over many years, not including the extensive provision of Home Care services for the terminally ill.

Symptom management, including pain control, is part of the holistic discipline of good palliative care which will include drug treatment, anaesthetic procedures, neurological approaches and psychological support.

Education and training

Education and training in Palliative Care is increasing in the medical undergraduate and post-graduate programmes and the Association for Palliative Medicine has produced guidelines for the teaching of the specialty at all grades. The Royal College of General Practitioners and the Association for Palliative Medicine have issued a joint statement which sets out an appropriate syllabus for medical students, General Practitioners, hospital doctors and specialists in the field. These are now widely implemented in teaching programmes and in post-graduate sessions, which doctors are now encouraged to attend as part of the Continuing Medical Education initiative.

Communication

In addition there is an initiative from the General Medical Council to incorporate training in communication in this and other fields, at an early stage in the undergraduate curriculum. Many of the difficulties in this area of care derive from deficient communication between patient and doctor, patient and relatives, relatives and professional carers as well as between relatives and patients. There is much advantage in free discussion of the issues from a basis of openness and honesty between all the people involved, provided this is done in a sensitive manner.

'In 1992 the UK had 183 in-patient Hospices already established.'

Nursing training and education

In Scotland there is a heightened awareness of the need to provide quality education in the field of palliative care and in the care of the terminally ill. There is more input than in previous years to the 'Project 2000' Nurse Education programme and there are several courses available at post-registration level.

This does not, of course, guarantee the quality or the direction of such education, and it is noted that there are some influential people in VESS whose voices are likely to be heard in determining these issues.

Courses

Courses and modules on Cancer Care and Palliative Care are run for nursing staff in various centres and Colleges of Nursing throughout Scotland including Glasgow, Edinburgh, Dundee, Aberdeen, Borders, Argyll and Clyde, Ayrshire and Arran, and Highland.

There are many opportunities for nurses to be educated in these topics and there are many groups and organisations willing to provide it. Many in this field, but by no means all, would adopt as a part of their ethos an acceptance of the principle of the sanctity of life. Similar concerns apply to the nursing response to legalisation as were noted with regard to doctors.

The caring anomaly

It is a curious situation that the demand for legislative change towards euthanasia should be so prevalent at a time when the necessity for such a draconian measure is so rapidly diminishing, as the means of relief become better appreciated and more available.

Provision of resources

Adequate supportive and palliative care is only possible if resources are made available for the patient, for the supportive family and for the General Practitioner in undertaking this type of care. These resources should include social and counselling support, as well as the relevant equipment, medication and personnel. In the National Health Service, this is a matter for Central Government, as well as for the local providers of care, and a degree of priority should be given to establishing and maintaining such provision. The need for palliative care should be considered as part of the Health Needs Assessment enjoined upon Health Boards and Local Health Authorities.

Research

Similarly, resources are required for the study of specific needs and for research into the development of symptom relief techniques. This research requires to be supported in recognised centres of good practice.

Increase in awareness of means of relief

As noted above there is much advantage in openness in talking about terminal illness. The conspiracy of silence between sufferer, carers and associates is an outmoded and destructive concept, but it tends to persist, especially among older people. Much can be done to dispel the mists of secrecy by a readiness on the part of the doctor or nurse to discuss clinical options, intentions and possible outcomes. There is a need for professionals to abandon their mystique in serious illness, especially as people become more aware of their own health and health-care needs, and this will require also an admission of the limitations of clinical care.

'The conspiracy of silence between sufferer, carers and associates is an outmoded and destructive concept.'

Publications and publicity

The proponents of euthanasia are extremely active in the production of literature, and in the publication of their ideas and proposals in the media. It is important not only to counter such arguments where they appear in print or on the air, but also to inform the public concerning the alternative and equally valid approaches to the difficult decisions at the end of life. The Church should not be engaged exclusively in criticism of the misguided; it should also be concerned to demonstrate a better way and a better approach to life's dilemmas.

CHRISTIAN ACTION
in caring for AT-RISK PEOPLE

It is not enough to oppose the progression of pro-euthanasia arguments, nor simply to oppose VES and similar bodies. If the Church is to say 'no' to euthanasia, it must be ready to say 'yes' to life-affirming alternatives. The Christian Gospel is a Gospel of HOPE, and, in particular, of hope in the context of death and hopelessness. In the situation of terminal care the challenge is to bring effective relief within this context of Christian hope. It has been characteristic of the Church through the ages that it has been in the forefront of work for the suffering, the dying and hopeless. The Hospice movement owes its existence largely to Christian initiatives which, while they have been followed by secular involvement, remain a positive motivation.

The roots lie in the need for Christians to do, rather than merely to protest. A belief in the eternal worth and dignity of human beings is the mark of the Christian since the Lord Himself gave the worth of His own life and death to each one and afforded us the dignity of His eternal love.

'The Church should not be engaged exclusively in criticism of the misguided. It should also be concerned to demonstrate a better way and a better approach to life's dilemmas.'

'If the Church is to say "no" to euthanasia, it must be ready to say "yes" to life-affirming alternatives.'

'It has been characteristic of the Church through the ages that it has been at the fore-front of work for the suffering, the dying and the hopeless.'

Where the elderly, the disabled, the dying and the dementing are held in respect as fellow human beings, they cease to be seen in negative terms. They also cease to be seen as an alien 'other' kind of person for whom the best thing is to give up on life, but are valued as individuals and to the Christian, as individuals for whom Christ died. To quote from Dr John Wyatt, a prominent paediatric specialist:

> *In summary, Biblical Christianity does not devalue individuals because of their disability. In fact, from a Christian perspective, all of us are disabled in some sense by the consequences of the Fall, and the differences between us are therefore only in degree. The essence of humanity is not in our functional ability, which may be impaired to a greater or lesser extent, but in our creation as beings made in God's image. Functional impairment in itself does not impair our dignity or worth as human beings. The central purpose of human life is seen, not in the selfish pursuit of pleasure through use of our bodily functions, but in mutual, loving relationships with others and with God Himself. In Christian terms it is these personal relationships of love and self-giving which give life its 'quality'.* (*Survival of the Weakest:* CMF publication)

Christian compassion demands active involvement, and Christ's words to His followers, 'in as much as you did it unto the least of these, my brethren, you did it unto me' (Matthew 25:40), should be sufficient motivation for them to be found among the practical carers for the disadvantaged, rather than merely among the protesters.

How do we go about caring?

1   By spiritual, emotional, intellectual and physical support for the sufferer and for carers, who may be themselves 'fellow sufferers'.

2   By defining needs of both groups (patient and carer).

3   By emphasising relationships involving patient, carer, professionals and God in the positive context of Christian HOPE. The Church can and should be taking this as a challenge since it is a matter of 'coming alongside to help'. 'Paraclete' (one called alongside to help) is the word for, and the work of, the Spirit of God. 'Bear ye one another's burdens, and so fulfil the law of Christ' (Galatians 6:2).

4   By consistent and practical support for care establishments.

5   By extension of the care principles applied in specialised contexts, to general hospital and home care and practice. Hospices and specialist care establishments are only part of the answer.

6   By visiting and supporting the terminally ill or disabled in their homes or in hospital, and meeting their specific needs as they become apparent. This is clearly as relevant for the individual Christian as for Church groups. Ministry to the spiritual needs of people in serious or terminal illness is as essential as the physical ministrations of medical or nursing professionals.

'Ministry to the spiritual needs of people in serious or terminal illness is as essential as the physical ministrations of medical or nursing professionals.'

7   The Christian home is also a resource which, perhaps, we may be too reluctant to employ. The Lord commended this to His followers with the words, 'I was a stranger and you took me in', as well as 'I was sick and you visited me'. The 'CARE' Homes programme addresses this concept and relief has been given sometimes to terminally ill people themselves, but, more often, to their carers who are in need of respite. The Good Samaritan is a further example of someone who while he did not use his own home to receive the injured man, did apply first aid and paid the hotel charges and the treatment costs.

8   It may also be very relevant to campaign and motivate those in local and national government to improve resources; to stimulate professional bodies and organisations to take an interest in symptom relief as much as in cure; and to demand a positive alternative to the so-called 'easy option' of euthanasia, 'masterly inactivity', or therapeutic nihilism.

BIBLICAL TRUTH
and the AFFIRMATION *of* LIFE

'No one can keep himself from dying or put off the day of his death. That is a battle we cannot escape; we cannot cheat our way out.'   Ecclesiastes 8:8, Good News Bible

Legalisation of euthanasia will not produce a solution to the needs of the individual sufferer; *or* address the health-care challenges of contemporary society. It is the expression of an attitude to life which belittles the sovereignty of God, diminishes the importance of sustaining relationships, and inhibits the pursuit of life-affirming answers for people in need and distress. Christians must be active in promoting positive alternatives derived from Biblical truth, so that the momentum toward intentional killing may be curbed. The Church of Scotland has an obligation before God to assert God's interest in life, rather than in death; to exercise Christian compassion towards the sufferer, the disabled and the dying; and to encourage the relief of symptoms and improvement in the quality of life for such people. The Church cannot support euthanasia as a means to any of these ends, and rejects the introduction of death as a treatment option in any clinical situation. Jesus said: 'I am come that they may have Life, and that they may have it more abundantly' (John 10:10). This declaration applies at the end of life or in the midst of distress, just as much as it does in any other circumstance, or any other time.

'Christians must be active in promoting positive alternatives derived from Biblical truth, so that the momentum toward intentional killing may be curbed.'

'The Church cannot support euthanasia as a means to any of these ends, and rejects the introduction of death as a treatment option in any clinical situation.'

APPENDIX 1:
STUDY GROUP MEMBERS

Dr George Chalmers, Consultant Geriatrician.

Mrs Ann Allan, Teacher.

Revd Robert Lynn, Minister.

Mrs Margaret Foggie, Solicitor.

Mrs Marjory Walker, Retired Social Worker.

Dr John Berkeley, Consultant in Palliative Medicine.

Revd Alistair McGregor QC, Minister.

Miss Kristine Gibbs, Social Worker.

APPENDIX 2:
ACKNOWLEDGEMENTS

Dr Derek Doyle, Medical Director, St Columba's Hospice, Edinburgh.

Dr John S Wyatt, Reader in Neonatal Paediatrics, University College Hospital, London.

Bishop A Haggart, Voluntary Euthanasia Society of Scotland.

Revd Dr A Stewart Todd, Theologian.

Drs R L J M Scheerder, Deputy Director of Health, The Netherlands.

Mrs Christine Thayer, Council of Europe.

APPENDIX 3:
EUTHANASIA –
RELEVANT EVENTS
in RECENT YEARS

1968:   Church and Nation report to General Assembly.

1969:   EXIT (Voluntary Euthanasia Society) aims to strengthen the case for active termination of life by conducting public opinion polls which appear to indicate that there is widespread support for voluntary euthanasia, and organised a public poll which claimed that 51% of the British public were in favour of euthanasia.

1970:   Euthanasia Society of America changed its name to 'The Society for the Right to Die'.

1972:   Euthanasia began to be practised in the Netherlands.

1975:   Committee on Moral Welfare reported to the General Assembly (p 352).

1976:   World Federation of 'Right to Die' Societies established.

1976:   Voluntary Euthanasia Society organised a public poll which claimed that 69% of the British public were in favour of voluntary euthanasia.

1977:   Church and Nation Committee report to General Assembly (p 119).

1980:   Voluntary Euthanasia Society published booklet, *How to die with dignity*.

1980:   Hemlock Society started in America.

1981:   Board of Social Responsibility submitted summary report to the General Assembly (p 301-302) (Deliverance p 26.20).

1983:   Royal Dutch Academy of Science and the University of Utrecht sponsored research about cases of involuntary euthanasia in leading Dutch hospitals.

1985:   Voluntary Euthanasia Society organised a public poll which claimed that 76% of the British public were in favour of euthanasia.

1987:   The National Opinion Poll indicated that 35% of doctors would be prepared to practice voluntary euthanasia were it legal.

1/1988:   Dr Colin Brewer, a British psychiatrist, told *Health Week:* 'We regard some people as not worth keeping alive and others as worth keeping alive'.

5/5/88:   Publication of BMA guidance on euthanasia.

2/6/88:   Gallup Poll on voluntary euthanasia for terminally ill patients: 66% of women said 'yes', 75% of men said 'yes', 20% said 'no', 10% did not know, 71% of old age pensioners said 'yes'.

12/8/88:   Voluntary and non-voluntary euthanasia accounting of 15% annual death rate in the Netherlands (*De Telegraaf,* Amsterdam).

1989:   Euthanasia decriminalised in The Netherlands.

12/89:   A Dutch doctor was formally reprimanded for refusing to practise euthanasia on a patient who had requested it.

1/90:   Early Day Motion tabled in the House of Commons for euthanasia.

8/5/90:   Voluntary Euthanasia Bill (put forward by Mr Boyes, as above): voting: For 35, Against 101, 510 MP s expressed no view.

7-10/6/90:   The 8th World Congress of Right to Die Societies, Maastricht. Dutch doctors performing euthanasia of patients with 'unbearable suffering' will not be prosecuted providing they report the death to the Police. The Chief Prosecutor no longer passes the cases to the Attorney General.

Dutch MP Mr Kohnstamm and Euro MP I van der Heuvel stated that euthanasia should be legalised in all the countries of Europe by (i) media exposure;

(ii) encouraging the European Parliament to move into a field of new health law; and (iii) getting discussions with the Council of Europe with the aim of encouraging the establishment of a 'Commission on the Rights of the Dying'.

4/91:   European Community Environment and Public Health Committee voted in favour of Voluntary Euthanasia by 16 votes to 11.

6/91:   European Parliament approved unanimously the document submitted by the EC Environment and Public Health Committee.

2/8/91:   All-Party Group on Voluntary Euthanasia. 90 MPs sympathetic to views of Voluntary Euthanasia Society.

16/8/91:   *Final Exit: The Practicalities of Self Deliverance*, published in USA. Sold 20,000 copies in two weeks.

9/91:   The EC Human Rights Commission stated that, 'Wherever a sick person in perfect clarity of mind demands strongly and persistently that an end be put to an existence which has lost all dignity for him, and where a committee of doctors convoked for the purpose recognises the unavailability of any further treatment', euthanasia should be granted.

19/10/91:   The Netherlands: 9000 explicit requests noted this year; less than one third are agreed; 3% of all Dutch deaths are from euthanasia; 62% Dutch GP s have performed euthanasia, 28% in the last two years, only 9% said that they never would. Reasons for patients asking: loss of dignity 57%, pain 46%, unworthy dying 46%, dependence on others 33%, tiredness of life 23%.

11/91:   Dutch study suggests doctors had killed some patients without their specific request on the grounds of the poor quality of the patient's life.

5/11/91:   Washington US Initiative 119, giving doctors the legal right to help mentally competent patients to end their lives if they are expected to live no more than six months, was narrowly defeated.

13/11/91: Sir Ralph Hoffenberg, past President Royal College of Physicians, at a Health-Care Policy Conference, advocated legal euthanasia for chronically sick pensioners. 'Euthanasia could be an alternative to sustaining poor quality life for frail, elderly people, providing it is in the best interests of the patients and their family'.

15/7/92: Draft Euthanasia and Hospice Bill presented as a Notice of Motion to the House of Commons.

16/8/92: Dr Cox terminated the life of Mrs Lillian Boyes with a lethal dose of potassium chloride.

16/9/92: *Daily Telegraph:* 'The abandonment of the Judaeo-Christian tradition which still underpins our medical ethics would alter the Health Service beyond recognition. Hospitals would no longer be houses for healing only. For the confused elderly, and the seriously ill, they would become places of fear.'

21/9/92: Dr Cox was given a 12 month suspended sentence for attempted murder of a terminally ill patient.

25/9/92: Dr Richard Smith, *British Medical Journal* editor, proposed the setting up of a Royal Commission on Euthanasia.

13/11/92: The High Court told doctors they would be committing murder if they took Tony Bland off his feeding tubes.

17/11/92: BMA: 'The deliberate taking of human life is against the law and we do not believe that law should be changed.'

19/11/92: The High Court agreed for Tony Bland's tubes to be withdrawn, but the High Couth Official Solicitor maintained that withholding food from Mr Bland would be tantamount to murder.

2/2/93: Five Law Lords decided that Tony Bland should be allowed to die.

5/2/93: The House of Lords authorised permission for medical staff to stop feeding Tony Bland.

6/2/93: The House of Lords established an enquiry into the ethical, legal issues surrounding euthanasia cases.

12/2/93: The Dutch Parliament voted to permit euthanasia under strict guidelines.

26/2/93: Michigan became the 29th United State to bring in laws against assisted suicide.

16/3/93: The Medical Treatment (Advance Directives) Bill was introduced in the House of Lords.

2/4/93: BMA Survey: 69% Consultants and 62% of GPs approved of the removal of life support treatment from patients in a hopeless coma after relatives have given permission. Four in ten doctors want to be free from fear of prosecution over such an action. Three out of ten support active euthanasia when a patient is in intolerable pain.

26/4/93: The National Opinion Poll, on behalf of the Euthanasia Society, published research that states 81% of Scottish adults think that they should be helped to achieve a peaceful death if they are suffering from an incurable, physical illness which is intolerable to them.

28/4/93: The Law Commission for England and Wales recommends that doctors should be bound to comply with Living Wills made by patients who later become incapacitated.

11/6/93: The MP for Southall withdrew his Ten Minute Rule Bill for Euthanasia.

31/1/94: The House of Lords Select Committee on Medical Ethics published its report on Euthanasia (Hansard).

APPENDIX 4: SELECTED BIBLIOGRAPHY

A Theological Perspective on Euthanasia: A Haggart (VESS, 1991).

A Time to Die: R G Twycross (CMF Publications, 1986).

'Acting or Letting Go: Decision Making in Neonatology in the Netherlands' in *From Cells to Selves: Ethics at the Beginning of Life:* E Van Leeuwan and G K Kimsma (1993), pp 265-269.

Death, Dying and Euthanasia: D J Horan and D Mall (eds).

Death without Dignity: N M de S Cameron (ed) (Rutherford House, 1990).

Do we have a duty to die?: J Beloff (VESS, June 1987).

The Dying Patient, R W Raven (Pitman Medical, 1975).

The End of Life: J Rachels (Oxford University Press, 1986).

Ethical Responsibility in Medicine – the Christian Approach: Edmunds and Scorer (E & S Livingstone, 1967).

'Euthanasia': BMA Working Party (British Medical Association, 1988).

Euthanasia in the Netherlands: The State of the Debate: C Thayer (Council of Europe).

Euthanasia – Spiritual, Medical and Legal Issues in Terminal Health Care: B Spring and E Larsen (Multnomah Press, 1984).

Facing Death and the Life After: B Graham (World Publishing, 1987).

Final Exit: D Humphry (Hemlock Society USA, 1991).

The Handbook of Medical Ethics: (BMA, 1981).

Medical Ethics and Human Life, D Braine (Palladio Press, 1982).

Medical Treatment (Advance Directives) Bill 1993 (HMSO,1993).

Medicine in Crisis: N M de S Cameron (Rutherford House, 1988).

The Morality of Killing: M Kohn (Peter Owen, 1974).

On Being Human: R S Anderson (Wm B Eerdmans Publishing Company, 1982).

Pediatric Euthanasia: J P Orlowski (et al), AJDC vol 146 (December 1992).

Survival of the Weakest: J Wyatt and A Spencer (CMF Publications, 1992).

Termination of Medical Treatment Bill 1993: House of Lords (HMSO, 1993).

When is it Right to Die? Euthanasia on Trial: J Eareckson Tada (Marshall Pickering, 1992).